New Zealand Endangered Species

LAND SNAILS

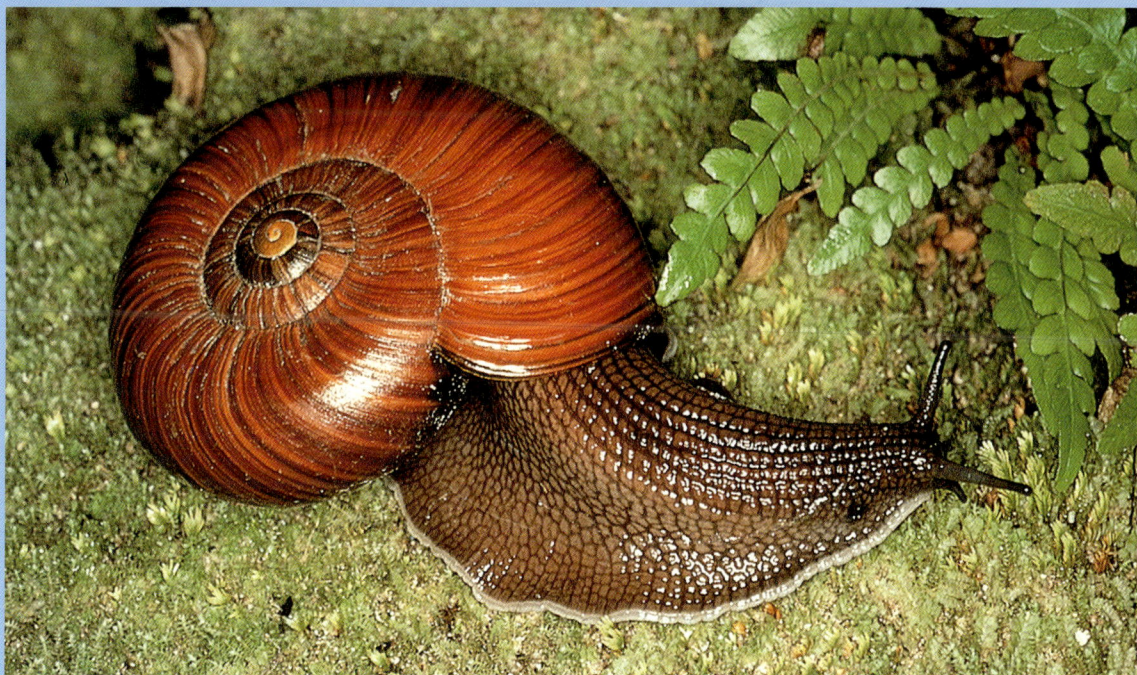

JENNY JONES

Heinemann
PRIMARY

Jenny Jones wishes to express her thanks and gratitude to Kath Walker, Fred Brooks and Ian Stringer for their expertise and comments.

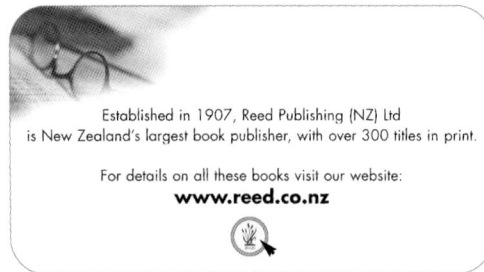

Established in 1907, Reed Publishing (NZ) Ltd
is New Zealand's largest book publisher, with over 300 titles in print.

For details on all these books visit our website:
www.reed.co.nz

Published by Heinemann Education, a division of Reed Publishing (NZ) Ltd,
39 Rawene Rd, Birkenhead, Auckland.
Associated companies, branches and representatives throughout the world.

ISBN 1 86944 449 3
© 2001 Jenny Jones
The author asserts her moral rights in the work.

Book design by Nicole Merrie

First published 2001

Printed in New Zealand by Brebner Print Ltd

CONTENTS

THE SPECIES

You can find land snails in lots of places, but not all are native to New Zealand. Some of the common snails that you find in gardens were introduced from Europe.

In New Zealand we have some amazing and interesting land snails that are not found anywhere else in the world. They are part of our unique fauna of invertebrates (animals without backbones).

In the past, when New Zealand was covered in forest, it had more than 1000 species of land snail. Their sizes, shapes and colours changed slowly (evolved) over time. But now, with much of the forest gone, many of the surviving land snail species are very rare.

Land snails, like other native species such as tuatara, weta and some frogs, are among some of our most ancient animals. They have been in New Zealand for millions of years and this makes them special.

New Zealand land snail shells

Land snails come in a huge variety of sizes. They range from those with tiny shells about the size of a pinhead, to giant species with shells the size of a person's hand.

The tiny land snail species are so small they do not even have common names. They live within damp forests in rotting logs and on branches of trees. This is where they find the leaves and fungi they like to eat. The shells of the tiny land snails have beautiful ridges and lots of spikes all over them that curl this way and that.

Some of the giant species are the Marchant's snail, the kauri snail and the flax snail. The superb snail is the largest of all!

Not only are they large, they are also heavy. They can weigh 200 g or more — about as heavy as an orange! They grow slowly — some take about 15 years to become an adult and they can live for up to 40 years.

Introduced land snail

APPEARANCE

Land snails are part of a group of animals called molluscs. This group also includes other soft-bodied species, such as slugs, sea snails, octopus and squid.

The land snail has a soft, flat, fleshy area called a foot. It is made of muscle and is very powerful. Snails 'crawl' or move around using this foot. On a damp night some land snails can travel more than 200 m. That is quite a long way for such small animals.

Snail showing its foot

Kauri snail   Flax snail

On the front of the snail's foot is the head. This is where the senses of touch, smell and sight are found.

On top of the foot is the shell that protects the snail's very soft body. The shell grows as the animal grows. Different species of land snails have different shaped and sized shells. Some, such as the flax snail, have a long, pointy shell. The superb snail has a large, round, flat shell. The kauri and superb snails have beautiful shiny shells.

If the snail is attacked, it can pull its foot and head into the thick hard shell for protection. Snails' eyes are on the end of stalks on top of their heads. They do not 'see' like we do, as they can only sense the difference between light and dark.

Some snails also have other shorter stalks on their heads that act like a 'nose'. Snails have an amazing sense of smell.

Their mouth is at the very front of the head.

So how do land snails breathe? Instead of a nose, snails have a breathing hole on the side of their foot, just below the shell.

Inside their bodies, snails have all the different organs an animal needs to stay alive. They have a stomach, a heart, kidneys and blood in blood vessels just like ours except they are 'snail sized' and work a little differently!

Snail blood is not red but ranges from clear to brown, green or even blue!

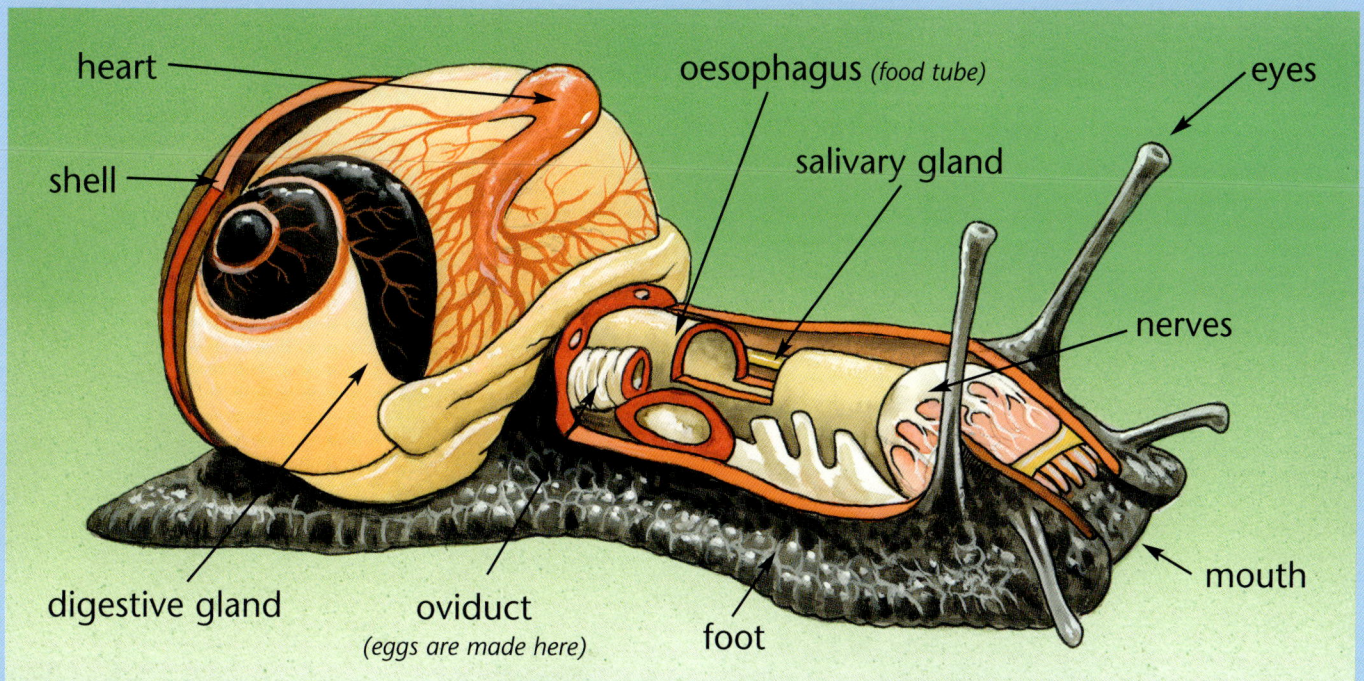

heart

oesophagus *(food tube)*

eyes

shell

salivary gland

nerves

digestive gland

oviduct
(eggs are made here)

foot

mouth

EATING HABITS

Land snails eat a variety of foods. Some, such as the flax snail, eat leaves in the litter layer of the forests. Others are carnivorous, eating only live animals, such as earthworms. They do this just like we eat spaghetti, starting at one end and slowly eating away until they get to the other end. Some also eat slugs and other snails.

Inside their mouths, snails have rows and rows of very tiny, sharp 'teeth' called radula (rad-u-la). The snail uses these teeth like a file, scraping them backwards and forwards to break off pieces of food that they can then swallow.

Giant land snail

Hochstetter's snail

HABITAT

The common garden snails make 'snail trails' from the silvery slime they leave behind. This slime helps to keep the snail moist so it does not dry out and die. However, many of our native land snails need to live in wet forests to survive as they do not make snail trails and dry out really quickly. Living in your garden is not a good habitat for these land snails.

They need to live in the leaf litter in the forest, and some need to live on the mountains where it is cool and damp. These forests do not dry out like the ones close to the coast. Many native snails are also nocturnal, only coming out at night to search for food. This also helps save them from drying out.

Powelliphanta

Fossil shells of land snails have been discovered in many parts of New Zealand. These fossils tell us where our land snails were once found and the fossil remains of trees found with the shells show us the types of vegetation that would have been there in prehistoric times. Back then, the habitat was more suitable for land snails and there were more species. Also, with the absence of predators, some species could grow much larger than they do today.

A number of fossilised land snail shells found were much bigger and heavier than those found today.

Oparara land snail

BREEDING

Land snails are not male or female, but both. There is no difference from one snail to another.

They each have eggs, and at mating time each snail needs to have its eggs fertilised by another snail. They do this using a small tube which they attach to the other snail.

Once this has happened, the snails then lay clutches of eggs in a nest — a scooped out area in the ground under the leaf litter. Some land snails, such as the flax snails, have soft-shelled eggs, while others such as the kauri, Marchant's and superb snails have hard-shelled eggs. So how do snails lay their eggs? They have an egg-laying hole in their neck!

The eggs remain in the nest during the winter. Sometimes more than one land snail will lay its eggs in the same nest. There can be about 20 eggs in one nest. They develop for some time depending on the species. Some like the flax snail can take anything from 6–16 weeks to develop, and will hatch any time between November and March.

Snail eggs in a nest

YOUNG

Young snails are called hatchling snails. They hatch out of the egg looking just like an adult snail, but smaller. They already have their first shell. Imagine how small some of the really small adult snail's hatchlings must be! You would need a magnifying glass to see them.

As they grow their shells grow with them. You can see the growth rings on the shell if you look carefully.

Young land snails start to move around in their habitat at night when it is safer and cooler. They take about four years to become adults.

Hatchling flax snails leave the nest and move up into the trees. They hide on the underside of leaves or deep in plants during the day for safety. They live here while they grow.

Giant land snail hatchlings live on the forest floor where they eat rotting leaves, and grow in the safety of the leaf litter.

PREDATORS AND DEFENCE

Land snails come in a variety of colours, which help to camouflage them in their environment. For the tiny ones, having spikes on their shell not only makes the snails appear bigger than they actually are but makes them difficult to eat.

Land snails, like any other animal, will survive as long as they can find the food they like to eat and plenty of shelter.

They have survived in New Zealand with their natural enemies — birds, such as the weka, piopio, adzebill and laughing owl — for a very long time.

Weka

Laughing owl

smallest snail

largest snails

0   10
mm

0   10   20   30   40   50   60   70   80   90   100   110   120
mm

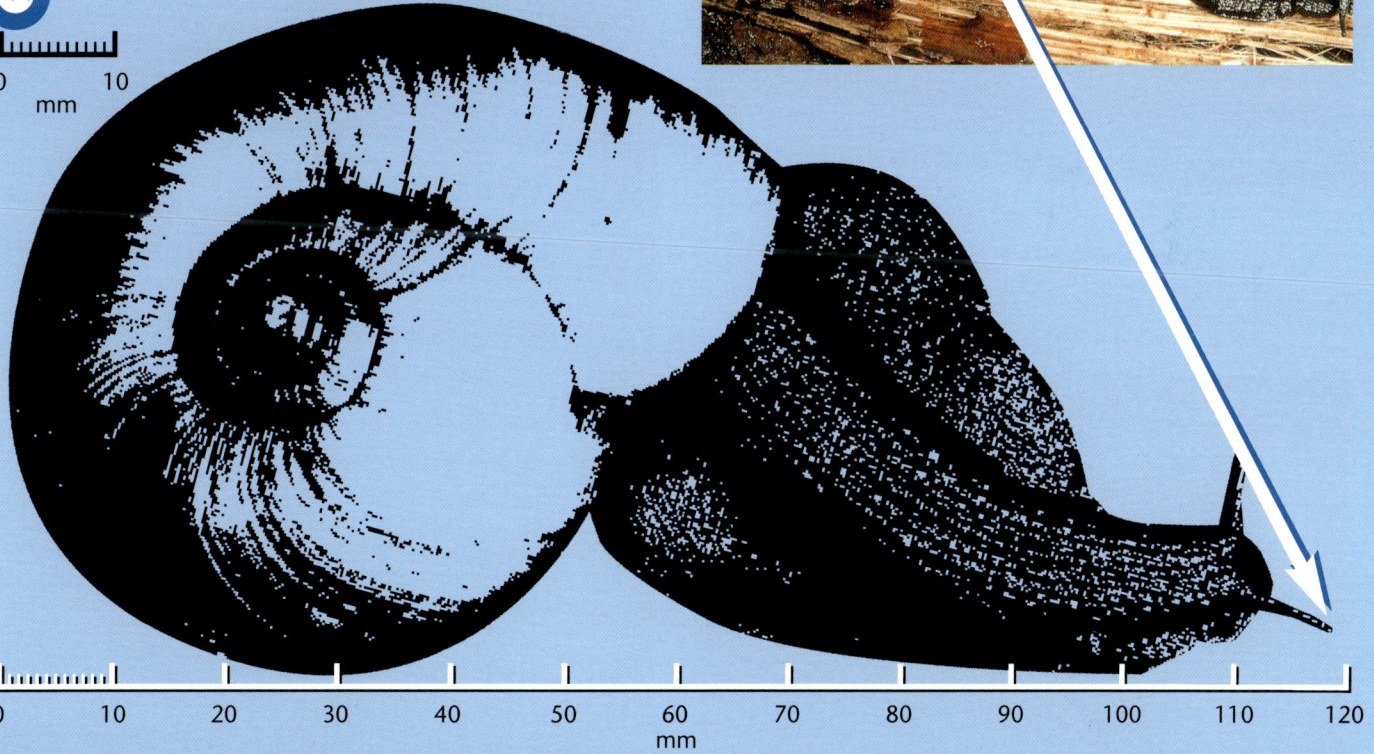

The smallest and largest land snails in New Zealand

REASONS FOR DECLINE

Today it is difficult to find many of our ancient land snail species. The clearing and burning of the forests by humans has destroyed the habitat of many land snails. For many species there are only small areas of the right kind of habitat remaining. There are also many introduced species, such as rats, pigs, hedgehogs, stoats, possums, thrushes and blackbirds, that all prey on our native land snails.

Cleared land

Hedgehog

These snail shells have been damaged by birds.

CONSERVATION

WHAT ARE WE DOING TO HELP?

Scientists are studying our native snail populations to find ways to conserve or protect them.

Many of our land snail species survive only in small areas in forests or on islands where they are more protected.

Many people have collected land snail shells. Sometimes there is still a live snail inside that they destroy. But living snails need the old shells to eat, as they provide calcium. Empty shells should really be left exactly where they are, so all our native snail species, from the amazingly tiny to the giants, are able to continue to slither through time.

FACT FILE

THREE ENDANGERED LAND SNAILS

Flax snail

Flax snails often live in flax bushes but flax is not their main food. They are found in the warmer, northern parts of the North Island near the coast. They prefer forests where there is salt spray from the sea.

Flax snails are nocturnal (active at night) and feed on moist fallen leaves. During the day they often hide under the leaf litter. They have a long, pointy shell and when fully grown the shell can weigh 17 g and reach a length of 115 mm.

They take about four years to become an adult. In the winter, they lay 6-mm eggs in a nest in the ground under the leaf litter. More than one snail will add its eggs to the same nest. One nest could contain as many as 30 eggs.

In spring, the eggs hatch and the small snails climb up into trees to live on the underside of leaves. They do not return to the ground until they reach 10 mm and their shell is too heavy to stick to the leaves.

Flax snails have become endangered because their habitat has been destroyed, and they cannot hide from predators such as rats, pigs, blackbirds and thrushes.

Kauri snail

The kauri snail is also known by its Maori name, pupurangi. It lives in leaf litter and under grasses and ferns in the forests of northern New Zealand. Kauri snails have a thick heavy shell that is up to 75 mm across. Kauri snails grow quite quickly, reaching adult size in seven years, with the shell doubling in size from five years on. They are carnivores, feeding mainly on worms, and can travel distances of 200 m or more on wet nights.

Kauri snails lay 4–6 oval-shaped eggs, that are 10–13 mm long, in a hollow underneath the leaf litter on the damp ground.

Having a thick, hard shell helps protect the snail from some predators, but not all. Birds, rats, wild pigs and hedgehogs eat snail eggs and snails. These predators and loss of habitat have made the kauri snail an endangered species.

Superb snail

As its common name suggests, this is one of the largest of our species of land snails, and the shell can grow to more than 100 mm across.

Today, its habitat is limited to the high land and forests north-west of Nelson, where it lives in damp leaf litter. Superb snails are nocturnal and carnivorous, eating worms and other soft-bodied animals.

The superb snail's habitat is destroyed by introduced animals, such as goats and deer, that eat the saplings and smaller plants on the forest floor. The snails are eaten by possums, rats and the native weka, kaka and kea.

INDEX